SELF-PORTRAIT AS THE SPACE BETWEEN US

TRACE DEPASS

[PANK]BOOKS

Printed in the United States of America

First Edition
1 2 3 4 5 6 7 8 9

Cover Design by Io Escu
Interior and cover design PANK

Library of Congress Cataloging-in-Publication Data

ISBN 978-1-948587-03-7

PANK Magazine
PANK Books

To purchase multiple copies or book events, readings and author signings contact awesome@pankmagazine.com.

SELF-PORTRAIT AS THE SPACE BETWEEN US

TRACE DEPASS

Dedicated to: Howard DePass, each bridge he left,
his wife,   my great-grandmother, Granny, Jean,
and all their children, Diane, Denise, & Craig DePass;
and to my younger brothers, Chuppy, Dan, whom I love;
and to my grandpa, Wadell Wells,
and to my mother, my father, & the systems which
separate us all,
but brought us here, this new group home
wherein there is no time to dream   but dreams.

TABLE OF CONTENTS

[requiem] for the boy telling of the time his body was not his

who asks me   "what does this make me?"   but only asks me "should i have
regrets? cause i don't,"   who too hears   the sweet siren of train track that i know
all too well,   there's no shame   in those days where God does not act-
ually exist.   you ain't less
            than the boy you were before and neither of you died

            then, you know:
            you can hold breath, hold your nose, close your mouth

            and still hear
            the sound of a knuckle crack and, so, you are still, here.

            with a dap,
            before the goodbye that he is far too comfortable

            with saying,
            i try to make him feel that we are too young to be/   unmade
                                                                                            here.

                        and i say

                                    i'm glad you're here, man
                                    &   ...i love you, bro,
                                    & hit me up when you get to
                                    your crib,   & when he
                                    does get there, my phone
                                                            rings.

requiem for the butterfly effect

monarch's butterfly tripped over its wings
or walked with shackles
shushing itself to swallow sustenance
like the rest of them, vittles and now skulls
become Earth's nectar.
[i took one step forward, then two steps back]
out of dancing on death's toes. we don't flinch.
we departed that...
left Africa for white-washed wooden ships,
rotting, with dead folk and repetition,
no God. no witness.
i saw the butterfly that held my fate
(and realized that the ship is still buoyant,
it did not matter,
there are no options besides our own death…

and it was likely i would walk the plank,
watching water become my audience,
and spit me back out,
where the dead used to sing & had a song
like all the rest of them, i am still *here*,
making a habit
out all my nerves, most left not long after
we had left that land. left it for floorboards,
purpled with black blood,
green men with gray bullets and no mothers.
when i was about to plunge off that plank
i thought i would jump
whether it be with, or without, dead weight,
still don't matter. we would all become slaves,
soon, if not then late).

lament of the slave who does not jump

dogs from the dark do not carry
a name like 'appendages' for our
extensions of   self. i cannot tell you
exactly how dark   because how do dogs
put this dark in our mouth & hand it
to you without   language dark as english?
falling, or about to   , each time i blink
i only know that no one would hear me.

it was so Black in our basement that
when i'd fall i didn't know for how long
. i just know *good boy* has feelings - i slept,
splintered, climbed up what i assumed
was a 'mountain terrace' that would lead me
                                    to me
outside a body in dark, &   woke with
a fresh new gash in   me. the 'wood',
if not   'blood' itself,

                                    reminds me
                                    us dogs
have certain questions for the self
& mortality once we fall.

i sniff out   Black & questionable dogs.
if someone stared enough to know beyond
the past of my crooked canine to simply ask me
this question
                  Why   you play
so   aggressively, boy? i'd say
                                          i guess
my 'appendages' & saliva stay so pressed in
disagreement against your small
because i need to know for certain that
something is tangible enough to be
walked on here. i dip myself anywhere
like how human boys do   to test water
& you are the one who has given it
the name 'play'. i just need it to feel like
i'm digging for, at least, a name. i guess
if i could   imagine   heaven for dogs

as reparation, it would land, smackdab, during dogs'

about-faced fall, mountainside, up to the
sky & to atop of endless names, & there you hold
names like "hands" for those who keep my
wet nose away from "hands", each name still yours.
i guess one might say, to bring it   concise,
i "play" expecting the dark of your mouth
to give me, at least, names for   part of me.

& if they asked me   *Why do you not leave*
  ground, boy?   *it's   be   cause*
     i'm   too   scared   to   ask
Who   'ground' is?   What do
                                    'grounds' do?
how does   'ground' function?   how are we
so sure there is a 'ground' Who will bring us
back to these four   who keep us up?

if
        'ground' hurt me, then it
is not 'ground' that has kept me up,
i would say, but dogs from the dark
don't bark.   just play-crawl.
                   just teeth-love
                   here. perhaps

i could call you "mine" &   you could call me
"mine." perhaps, in english, it means we still
have   when we cannot see what was,
            or   could have been, ours,
                rather,

**requiem for colored boys who have considered jumping off the
Brooklyn Bridge & To   an eternal wave of depression when Mick
Jenkins "Waters" Mixtape wasn't enough,**

each hand is a cliff sieving the Niagara Falls from it's perfect, leaking-from-its
cracking self & could still smack a cup of heaven from my mouth & i know this because
all my aunts' knuckle. yet, the intent of the one hand writing this poem is not my
undeniable flinch, the smirk treading behind, nor the passive will nor wind of some
God's religion which gave hand to that genocide but,
this water healthy

how every black thing *here* living: feels it's truly alive because it has chosen to
float or has deliberately gone   too deep, wherein the blue lies in
the literal sense, *here,* we, the truly living, know these blues to be a happy li[f]e
so lost within today's date's air, it could only be a reflection of the times &
spaces   &   on the other hand are deep
                                              sadder colors, if we unstitch
                                              the globe of its old made-up
                                              margin lines & see all its sea

          inside-out, from the top, diving
          down, from: its truth of burgundy
          to: beneath tears too fragile to
          have had the strength to
leave. & so, if there's a God unwilling to unearth my billows of shame, if it could
bring me my tears livid enough to have become done
away with me, this way, you'll see
nothing "earth" remains

a true blue   (. the light you presume is, is as lost & stagnant as this is, all the while
                under us/the earth dives into self so thunderously/ it agrees with the cosmos):
                                    the farther you go
                            redder you become,
                                until you are both
                            black & invisible. & you
            don't even have hands to seek out
something you don't blend in with. watch: black wave until you
got the names of subtly new colors. & that, to us, people of shade that was once
color(s), is a God-like introspection: how we can   look out
                    from nowhere & believe we see: a fire of reds
so blues-drunk, it knocks down all it ain't once ask to touch
& yet we only see the self.
& yet to only see the self, in the mi(d)st of each metaphor for a nearing death
might be finding a thing which makes us stay
    afloat, a blues, a
light unwilling to redshift. &   to project our drowning on to the water
might be keeping us from the death itself.

silence

there you are, trying to take a nap and not napping
with all countless things:
a college application, a poem, a homie
on dialysis

you wish there was another person put in this place,
besides these voices

and spirits once squished together, /   in this train cart of a bedroom,
readying for an eternal drum circulation, /   with the volume down,
reeking of an unanswered prayer /   and never to reach up again,
that sound like blood of a fed-up black boy /   ...

it sounds like something burning *here*. /   *is some shit burning?*
though, you wouldn't know /   even if it had come from your kitchen,
holes in your pocket /   due to them late fees stacked by the oven
from last months' /   or coming from your own spit because you are just the

realest rawest rap /   hands down, realest, rawest, rapper [burning] alive here,
still gassed up off all these singles. /   still, no one hears this smoke rising.

it sounds like someone's hallucinating /   jaundiced delusions of grandeur,
and them' butterflies /   magnetized into your fridge door,
that gotta chance to fly up outta *here*, /   sound like hunger and tears forming,

the sound of just one hand, clapping, /
but, it is God *here* in some way /
just indifferent /

and it sound like everything had-happened
from the heavens, yet /
it was as if nothing was vibrating loud enough.

nothing, in all this *here* silence, /
knew what /
you know, /

truthfully. we, *here*, only know
that whatever it was, was black.

or waving to God,
just watching,
over death of fed-up black boys /

all at once,
from space.

not a thing
kept you up tonight.
it might have been you,

open letter to Dymel

i've asked too much of the sunset.
but, that wasn't my only sin.
it started after i was six and boy
was an arbitrary thing.

time - a construct, or figment of imagination,
affected by an elevation.
the top bunk paused time, be what i'm saying.
at least for me, that's what it did.

but i ain't know what it did for Dymel.
he, the other one
of the setting, sun, by my lap
he now moon across

and he *cosmos* for me. stars got jealous,
when i laid me down to the lucid sleep.
i don't know why i have this fond.
i was going just thru my compartments.

i miss that.
back when my body didn't come with rules,
innocence was still innocence
and stuff. remember?

it was when time was real real slow
and impossible ain't once forbade us.
ain't no mountain was high enough.
it's funny:

the higher we go, harder it is to truly breathe
as if we were really getting closer to heaven.
i'm close enough to tongue when gods gave me
Dymel and begged i repent for my identity.

i knew the night be too good to be true.
but, i remember the sunset.
although, she may not admit it,
i loved God better when i was mad young.

voyeur of voyeurs

mother told me religion too organized. said 10 commandments was cool though.
she said
those the things   you learn   to be true.

i said maybe the virtues. they a'ight. they could stay. said not every father should
be
honored like that, like: *what if he ain't there?*

mother taught me i was all of her & nothing like my father. taught me *handsome*
but nothing like my father. i was my mother's first love. & nothing like my father
gone. & can't "voyeur", the word, slip boys thru to the kind of father that is that
father too? don't the sound pucker the lips to a forced letting go? *& yes, the word
did. & if not,   speak it.*

mother nearly broke out the word *"voyeur"* as it sung all the baby teeth out of my
gums. i saw her point at it just this one time while she saw herself in it – ain't i tell
you her finger once jammed itself   in the word *"voyeur"*, like a God, & it would
not let go of what happened? & she still there, *like* ain't that like a God: to be both
still & *there?* &

unheard from. mother said she forgets but don't forgive.
        i often forget God like   men i don't forgive   too
        so i understand
                her. that's real.

i forget that i'm not talking to other men when i'm talking to myself so i
often forget which man i am.   or am in conversation with.   my mother taught
me i was all her. & no father.   mother taught me when the God that a father
can be leaves, you are both finished & unmade. & i had be my first love too. i
dreamt i

could be lovable again to someone before i began to love with someone else.
& ain't it the kind of alone only good God could grasp to then leave you lonely
with? that is where i was. that's where. like my mom, i don't leave. i've pointed
at it &, yes. the world spun around me.   but, nahh, not really. look - i weigh in
grams

mass of men i've been   abandoned to dust by
before all my own remainder   flesh, i think. not sure
how much exactly   this weighs or how much
world it takes   for this: man's shadow

16

to dislodge
the trapezius
out of my shoulder.
mother had told me
not to forgive a

[metaphor for going]

kind of a father
whose father, like him,
had gone but i'd forget
        about him
like how my mother
does &. how alike
my
grandmother *does* *watch*

~~friends say that i should inquire about~~
my father's isolation & ~~i should~~
~~ask him why he need to fly off a l o n e~~

            ~~all the time.~~
father's escape erodes a tree to its narrative
of rings, becomes his answer. blackbird - ready to listen
for a dad who would precede him in the nest &, yet,
all that, beneath his absent-reason for *why he gone?*
becomes Darwin's finch. competing for life worth living
as the stomach ache for word that is, was, or will be,
"*bond*". wherever the heavens' gate
gapes a beak to feed,   a storm comes   to fill
me. i get overwhelmed by this shower & forget
            to find tears for the bones unmade

like twigs by the *aim*!
            fire! thunder of gray stratus
in this moment,   billowing clouds
of silence. (*look*!) burned go my mother's wings up in it.
st(r)uck by rainfall, (*i don't know*) making   dead
birds question that which they heard. &   dead birds of
a feather flock. & they mock my mother's hesitance
together. they laugh but, i get her. i loves her. i've
            inherited her flinch at those that say
they gon "*fly*,"   yet they'll "*...return.*" i tell mom,

            i can't be here to mosaic
whichever promise that my father
            left inside as shrapnel,
but i want to so, moms, open up at least a mouth
for me on his behalf. i say/i need. just tell me
of father's escape he can't retain, or keep to him-
self ... & even after i'm piled of feathered bone
dancing into dust, i still might not find "enough". but,
at least i have truth. i don't know   (*who knows?*) whose promise
my father made to her although

            i did make sure to keep searching for it,
for whomever needs them a man.   i claw & dig away with wings   & ,
like God inside this nest, i unearth gray stratus   clouds,   again.   &   decades
worth of mists escape me like
this: his myths, his broken promise.   i bite, chew, grit through

18

where thunder emptied its archives in my home/nest/twig
like:

> *"wow. was this a cage that i bit too? oh.*
> *is this want to be man enough for you*
> *how my birdbeak mistakes its own birdcage*
> *for stubborn twigs? was it bad dna*
> *that st[r]uck as storm & let blood somersault*
> *across my body? this whole time? this why*
> *i was born unmade? because since birth i*
> *was thrown in a cage wherein not a thing*
> *in it rattled like a parent's love? how?*
> *did my father think i was a Phoenix?*
> *are these his ashes he forgot in me,*
> *or am i burning? & is that a lock?*
> *i only know five answers for certain..."*

1. i am not just my father's Phoenix.

2. home must be wherever we kiss to keep warmth in   & shut the smoke
    out.

3. neglected & abandoned are fires that could only be manmade. & then.

4. this is why some any mother   would   call   her baby's saliva
    vaseline - a thing
    must protect the skin from crisps because some boys' wings got
    to hurt more, burn better, than birds.

5. lightning. who knows if it's *what he left me?* or *why he left?*   her? but if
    my father's answer
    for *why he gone?* had a name, it would be lightning. what else could it be? i
    too am so afraid of lightning that i fly away.

open letter to Capital Steez

i think i dreamt i was a packed suitcase
already leaving
when i just got here,
anywhere since you
left i just wake up to white men,
don't know how they're *here*,
but know
this body hunts for joy
even when the eyes are closed   &
nothing except God
wants to turn the music down low
here. i get ready
with all the scantrons,
quiet shrapnel shards,
and the postage stamps
to be that person
throwing you to the teeth of another
they can't see me *here*.
i'm invisible
as they kick me out
my breastbone
eviction notice
be reason why the anywhen is when
i've wished to exit & was near the door
i know

   how this city so big
   it make you alone
   how we never look
  for each other inside the eye

   how nothing i'd say
   would ring home enough
   to make you stay and i still don't
   know what makes any difference

between "thank you" and "i'm sorry."
all i know is *today makes four*
years going on...   *forever,*   *Love/*
                                        Brooklyn

20

tonight's agenda for the codependent lover:

(Time:) When it's time to go
Will the hour know all our infinite names? If I give
the hour the truth it's heard from everyone but me,
will the hour call me at least my first name? I know
what I do here is a choice & what I do with a choice
is just a matter of time. & I choose. To let the
happening of things do what it does for a living. &
at least I own this much. If God is love, I know

if loving - only to then relinquish love so that I
can be loved that much again - feels like: not acting
on a want - a stillness unsure of itself in these
moments of silence; a death (of choices): I will have
to relearn how to
love
love.   I am reminded by the sun - we dream most
nights, alone in different houses. I forget she's as
still here as a broken clock. Even before her eyes
open, I dreamt she dreamt of the bodies that loved me
last & her own body, making a kiss. Even while she
dreams inside my dreams, I tell her I only dream I'll
learn to love to say Goodbye. I know

a boy like me run so much, the shackles around the
pronoun "us" undo into death & then dust. But,
if she said to me   give me at least something
warm to hold onto tonight, then I knew my house was
hers. I knew   If she wanted to leave for anywhere
but here, I would pull each of my body's buttons
apart with her name, yet I still oscillate between
forgiving & not being here like a God fumbling with
its own name stuck between its fingers;

with her, unfurled into a dream within my lap
I speak at a reflection in the back of her necklace If
love is blind, I'mma meet it halfway.   I
brought my eyes to sleep in search for that joy.
so,
(Time:) when I would not give me to my own idea of
death:
To death, I gave this: Process.
To Process, give this pronoun: i.

To you, I give i. To i,
Here's this[: want that, will learn that, &
                        heal].

(Time:) Now,
        Can I learn to love the hour as I would love
her as I want to love myself as I would want to give
love? If I learn to love the hours I loved her & still
love, how come only the hours promise to stay? & when
they leave me, will I remain a passive boy? I know
the unveiling of time is more enough than I'll ever
be & douses in the blackest dream what we're too much
to remember. I'll fill this hour up at least with a
thing I once loved & the next. & to that next love,
I'll listen. With intent
                to understand, although I may never
fully grasp this giving. & to a new love's locket,
I'll ask   Am I not too afraid of my wounds for
me to want to be here like I want to want (while I
still have time)? & to want, I'll give a considerate
thought, hope, & then act, if it means I know I'll be
loved again [in the morning's hour]...

        no matter how dark I am here & there,
        no matter how much light I feel I need
        no matter how much she says I'm "a dream"
        no matter how much I try to wake her up
                with my open mouth...

(Time:) From within a different poem, room, self…
[She hears this like the narrative of water.]

She says   take my hand, boy.
pull from here enough so that
you are so full
you once thought you
were drowning but,
know now you were not,
& you wake up from death:

& kiss(es) him, her, whoever you is, yourself. She
says for you, I love you, okay? I mean it.
(TIME:)   N/a
                [Insert description of Event] [...]

against the labor of talking

before the electoral vote,

my love returned to its body,
i glance at my male
galloping outside after dusk,
like unsolicited oceans;
after inertia handed me palpable silence,
my "boy" lamented
a bigger boy who still talks the same...
neglect happens as physical trauma:
a boy, abandoned by the one
who loved him at first,
assaulted him, & left him, &
apologized & assaulted him,
     whose father decamped.
forgive him, father   for whom or
why he does not know

   moving on.

what he knows,
might be guilt.
~~absence,~~

~~moving on.~~

after death,
another *being?*
[because -
to store-in

that _______ which
should never begin to begin,
its becoming, &
our refuting of it

after the first time it happened,

my memory discovered me -
nudged *here* to reclaim
the sound the flesh makes
a furled finger: wasn't a trigger before
i checked.
memory's flash becoming half ~~human,~~
i know,
now
whom he loved,
     that after they had
threatened him,
he might think he knows

    a love triggers its own body
  once its uneasy with its own
    "its own".

   as he thinks he knows,
tell him cast a ~~ballot for himself in (t)~~his

     ~~so he might know~~
~~& would~~ *love* despite redness when it aches.

 is its "boy" body

what is there
    from before that love
from that time
    which can't have begun;

    inside *whose room was it again?*
i should only look at the "now", i know
i must have just dreamt "boy" up,
   i must know
  ~~*"the one" as the prince of*~~
~~*peace, how they have both left*~~

~~& left again, so abruptly~~. *do i envy*   *lovers'*
envy? it discerns exactly & who
they are to forgive. & each time   *resolve? absolve? dispensation? exoneration?*
required another body
& each time -   *i* took
                                            each word, *defined them*

                 such that Time allows me a body
                 that is more me. survivor, *here,* at the
                         roundtable of trauma, know Love,
                         if anyone.   bodies where there lives
                 another body inside undead but
beautiful enough to be Autumn, hand Time
the handful of human more beautiful
than that

which — for whom it would not serve as
affirming of their body — *here's* god named *"how? how not?"*

i'm sure a ballot won't hold all this clicking quiet
    . it might leave[each room with a man in it   scratching its own walls,
       might drive each machine a god operates   out its mind].

when black men want to leave

we heard the asthmatic baby cry when the door shut. we heard the
bullet shell and body drop at the same time from miles away;
heard you; that he was too busy to finish [or start] the note that
he left us. heard him complaining about how much he didn't like
it, *here*. heard this place smelled like how his day went. that was the last time
we heard from him. there's a special kind of silence when black men leave.
we all thought it was him being himself and that he'd reappear, like
he always does. we all looked at each other, hoping we could pet
a stray tear back to it's duct, with words. but, we all struggled for some
thing good enough to say. throats got heavy. you could swallow and drown
in your own spit a few times when black men leave. mouths gape a whale's wail
and flood themselves. it tastes like nothing new. how there are such good things
we, perhaps, could say to make him stay that a mouth wouldn't utter.
if he only knew how much we wanted him home and happy and

our black man. now, a gone one. *here:* it;
                   the dusk, it rained all the way to dawn. none
                   spoke. we were tired and still drowning, watch-
                   ing the pitter-patter move in on us.
                   how water taunts us with it's large bodies
                   when we try to look for something besides
                   ourselves. what a gluttonous, gluttonous
                   God. looked so natural, it nearly made the son
                   want to be just like his father as though
                   to be taken to gone, gone for good,
                   was, for them, some hereditary thing.

self-portrait as the space between us

these days i just watch
                         them take the room inside their body
              when they're center-stage,
which means   they walk into the room like gravity, or
         the room, itself;

my body disarms
                         my head to paint my assailant as the silhouette
              on my right,
in the black box theater.   but i once found them as beautifully
                         drawn. & imagine
if everybody around us
                         knew it: a black hole as a self-
              portrait; them as a
dark brush against my   canvas, cracking it open, 'til i was
         devoid of some uniquenesses

but not of my Black.   i was the reaction to the room Black resides in,
              a rewinding Black
body sitting in the present   whose body once adapted to veering
              under my red light

                    of triggers
         in a play about power: this misreading of *no*
         even in english becoming creole of silence,
         unending of "self", the self (*but for whom?*)
         objectiveness objects, "his" [name - the congregate
         of nouns known such that there was a subject
         in his education, *history*, wherein "he" was
         so much of the subject, his body was considered
         biased, relative if not subjective, and could not be
         objective but, beforehand, a literal object, so much
         so, they skinned & scorched his whole name & "he"]
         became history - e.g.,

i, before i brush my teeth before the mirror, drag
my   parade of *history* to the back of my head,
         its tale of a pony, hogtied
         for my nappy black hairs in order

to look professional-like & "enough"
enough while the voice inside asks, as if *i* ain't me,

as if i'm guilty of my death,
as if *i*'m the only only only one the other side of who hurt me/alone,

with which
body, with whose autonomy,
with which right would he
continue to move? onto where?
& since his body was punctuated
male, why couldn't it   ?

the left side of the cerebral cortex colors the
right side of my room any shade i like
"right" to be, right when they walk into a
scene i happen to be inside, wherein they
have made their body center-stage of mine.

~~what i did with the space~~
the other day,

though single window inside
the bathroom tries to shatter out itself,

i do enjoy the shower – scorching, peeling the paint off his ceiling, literally.
    i unsheathe shed skin from the wall, now, of my own back.
    & paint over the wall several times &. efforts here
become undone more often than Youth's shoelaces. &,
at this point, i blame his paint for being
broken & not simply the boy
who might deserve a space that won't unstitch
itself under its own stretched sigh.
            paint
rips off its pants, cracks a smile, & i made myself to vacant room for so many
bodies so long that this room will learn to take, in kelvin, what i do to it with heat.
i know the air is homeless, too. it, all day, running like eyes throughout a painting
& is hot enough to see that there's
            nothing
that is truly enough to keep you living/here. mist
makes me wish to fleet passed this way -
              out
    that window. the word for this in english, i know, is *homeostasis*, or perhaps
in other words, *equilibrium*, & it brings a little death bit out a hot room
in order for people to say it happened & ain't
no longer, or never was. it's so people can laugh

still & not sink(s). my mouth adopted into english,
        like son to the grandmother he was not originally supposed to be son of.
        the language   carves, with faulty love, a home in the mouth
for each time i gather my hands enough to tell the mirror *how beautiful* it is,

a cough caught way passed the back of the throat
brings the body out the metaphor wherein it is its own room, back into the world
wherein my back be hunched in every room,
hawking up the sink's broken copper & diction, in
order to say to the black throat,   *whether import or export, any act of english*
    almost inflicts the same nuanced process of old deaths
so much so, the walls are painted   *involuntary*
blood; so much so, i am half-filled
english   *&*
    every indigenous/african tongue

slips out the windows of my body each anywhen
      we rap in the shower, or breathe.

              i laughed with a sink,
          the other day. *you ain't got no tongue...* my sink had laughed[
itself off of the wall. itself out of the hinge that glue can become & what was left
looked like an endless broken-ass jaw]. it took everything that i ain't ever
controlled, which i do still owe in late fees, to get it to quit laughing. & no one
asked me how i kept the lights on;
              how i could still speak.

when to (k)not

i hug her different.
i know not to sneak up on her.
my hands ask if she's comfortable.
they know when they are to ask twice

and i'd call it muscle memory.
i loved wrong before. now i know better.
i try not to dig too below the surface with lips.
i know not to be kissing bones often.

traumatized lovers taught me how to sing
refrains, how to be a dear in the dark,
and just be that there for her, how to cup
her earth so oceans don't runneth over,

       how to listen and just listen.
       she's given me her tour of self.
       here she points out which things we leave
       alone at night/   from the things we
          cultivate and/   water while   the sun's out.
                                          some days we love so
                                          good it hurts.
                                          some days we don't/

know.
some days
     she wants us to put a dent in a hill
     looking for the same trouble
     adam, eve, and them got into,
     right there beneath the precipice

     where white folks can't see
     all of our nooks and crannies
     laying, center-stage, in the unknowing
     of what we do now.

other days
     she would not even bring her bones this way.
     and i know now not to touch her
     when i ask *will we be okay?*
     i named this muscle memory.

how we keep time / during Kwanzaa

sometimes, drumming, i envy the drummer most often off of the
rhythm, sometimes listening to everyone outside himself in
order to grasp his own being. not the becoming of it, his
literal starting point on the axis on which he would die &
live & perhaps live on forever. "he," with his forced english, *here,*
negotiates his death with another kind of death as he lives,
whereas you must do this after you go & reclaim english: *run!*
[when you are truly alive,] *with muddied mind & memory* [your
forgotten rhythms across syntax becoming] *until there is*
no "until," just endless Time since you began it & this is how
we all know it would be: (h)ours. space: be weary of its children's
controlled demolitions so much so, by Winter, kids are their own
fathers, mothers, colonized & anxious children, staining our
drum with the redundant questions; wherein the wave itself worries
too of cycling its crests & troughs, especially the sounds now:
~~the character~~

in aforementioned "he"; he's a lot like creating a sound from
scratch: a new tide in the liquid inside a fountain wherein a
penny would dive into it head-first; a reaction unearthing
more precise reaction upon respiration, which would imply
earth exhale us any when? given we undid "Time", is it
that the fountain would still await what crashed as rusted & silver
coins in the way the drum might expect my palm to come home to it?
or would liquid, as its own agent, begin to move home?   when? i
hallucinate a tangible question, i imagine Time as
the only shackles i put back on once i hallucinated.
i imagine my mother, young, too *prey* to love my father but
loving him *ahead of her time*. i don't imagine my father
wanting to undo all the *her* of me over Time, i know it.
like the back of my hand knows the room around the skin of my drum

it be room full of my water. i imagine my rhythm is,
as the lead percussionist is, a mother, handing custody
of me as a baby over to my grandmother, displaced [how
our water might bend the light already refracting out from
this penny,] onto a vocabulary of music i do
not yet have. on issues *here:* if not for Winter, i'd not enter-

tain the difference between when i was tin with a bronze mask &/or
the wave from each epicenter each penny became. is there word
        for wading in waves of intangible things' inability
to die? maybe there's synonym for "through" but verb. maybe, if you
had to ask of other ba(n)d drummers, from me, you just might get non-e-
xperimental feelings that served as my answer, jealousy.
just that, for who they tend to be when they are not beings who live

        to fulfill the wishes of other human beings
        until… a fountain full of pennies, poem's image
        repeating in it-
                        self fleeting until…

        [the beginning.]

ode to nas / ode to the cousin the cousin of death

anesthesia & euthanasia, two
cousins in the night of killing, hand you
two wrenches like lilies for all the pain
first - one buds like a point with no axis
from which the second blooms   Fibonacci
spirals of petals which might cut any
other flower to the half-life. here, *with-*
in this act: the exact same corkscrewing
it takes to give a hand to a wrench, now,
euthanasia, like a cassette, rewinds
you to piles of nail, new york's, no home.
anesthesia is that baby still young
enough to be a want, at home, sporting
a children's toolbox, laughing, *anything*

[could be outside doors even death. look: here.]

the tesseract tethers rooms

if each room is a cube, if *here* perhaps is a room
this night i'll sit, stay, spin congruent with hypercubes.

                  yes, time, in cubes with a death in it, passes so fast
i could see all, even the deprived, of time, evaporate into a sky's black face.
is it transpiration once animals with human limbs depart earth as stray water?

allowance, adherence, allegiant s(p)un arisen
to hue from its own animal & then adhesion.

perhaps when a black body needs more time, something mass-
ive enough to be it lifts, from it, up.
perhaps when a black body needs   ,
minutes might chip away from it

                  or us; then, perhaps,
        dearbody, i knew never could i ever keep up.
everything, blackbody, which did not make me beauty enough, ran like a creek
thru
            me and coaxed oxbows not oxygen, just gin, from blood.
i had dreams of becoming for entire seasons a season back when i had dreams
                  & only Autumn.

                  ***

i depart my father's lids' dark & see: i barely recall light but please observe how
i was born how it is: to mourn.
the *it* itself, "mourning" mourning,
peering thru as it self,   seeing
& knowing
            here is no exit,
excavating, with deer eyes, *here*
            as *it*, only until the gradual *dying-it.*   the neon puss dye
in the rigged big, marred open, (a)jar from worms & dirt,
it reeks & itches like a house of too many nails,
burrowing its own white walls pink;
it looks.   like someone's entire incised, expired,
melonhead, *here* -- this collapsed underground underground.

certain places the dead still grasp
possess no place for the living & yet,

here might be but refurbished, repurposed,
a white ghost -- that cenotaph... *yours?*

my father's dog, found in the yard with a
bullet in its head, moved out *here*
where the belonged stray.

***

can't want to stay *here* without want.

am i too happy now to want   to marry something?   so   bound-in   by   its
dimensions, the love
        sets, resets by wind's direction & not intention?
is it just to(o) in the present? that's just   to(o) bad. hell, i might just love anywhen
else.
        so, no, not "my bad".
i tire of death, relative to me, not passing, in 3D. i need this divorce.
you go writ(h)e,
        go anthropomorphize rot incessant all   thru my body. look! there's
ceiling to this passivity: dirt. here's this room i've named --
                                        me.
outside that room lives just my other room,
                another cenotaph, maybe
                a separate cube,
which, after peering at it for long enough, i too
on some days become. watch: i've lost

track of my own tesseract face, mourning my spilled abandoned boy/hood. time
saddles, hastes, whips, leaves all at once. i get a few good looks at myself when a
lens   the other side

of me can tell me

how sharp
i look, in passing, in 3D.

this *here!* in a body who might soon forget me tells me of nuance in my will, how
this good letterhead tops my death certificate; how different i must be before she
felt

my hands, and, maybe, i like her
36

usage of time. the *it* within her knows
certain things before they happen.
perhaps, i'll make this place somewhere inside her all my
omnidirectional, omnitemporal, omni-
                    present at least thru
all my deerbody; my last, boundless & final place.

new american constitution / terms & conditions
after Terrance Hayes & Jorie Graham

the sunset's heat nudges an avalanche to bear-hug
      a deer until it converts, convulses, culverts to,
from its blood, several streams it would
      gladly drink from. ingredient: mandible of deer
will never screw-in, thru its own jaw, enough English
      to concur: the deer fear in its damp squeal
might incite, may excite, *let's say invite in* the snow.
      the snow, *mr. hayes*, too may not own teeth
but something caught in its taking nature
      something white, male, some-
thing that stampeded here before, taught me
      nations' soil reminiscences of men's incisors,
molars, forefathers. in regards to redlining, i
      disremember this brand of poverty, *acquiescence,*
its certain passivity knows to trail us, from black,
      red, translucent. in nature, doors are always open
or there is no door; a cave rejects bartering its
      being with men *but was its cliff Marxist?* whimsy blushed,
sloped down the brine of its deer's dark jawline,
      bleached stuffs under it — dark, with too many
legs to be men — to burnt sienna. & *who would know*
      how many nieces we lost to poverty & snow?
i, hovered me, choked me to *me*. i courted him once.
      &, a god, near us, from his coma, just woke his ass
up. in this avalanche, i am its snow.
      in this avalanche,   i am the deer *but who isn't?*

the deer unsuspecting that its cold-blooded killer
            won't be, it turns out, human. snow unsuspecting its
white sheets would wave not as surrender flag but, *here*, now:
            to whiteness conceding copies of, in fact, itself.

some poems, perhaps   *here*, perhaps
            not exactly *here*,
        as one and zero as a quark,
i'm not, by the end, killing myself. i simply ain't

expect
embracing
what revolves
to be this gruesome.
                only
        a god can see his blood, see its snow, be unwilling
to unsee, wake up from a coma, and see with deer
                            eyes, you,
                            and smile,
                            as though
                            nothing
        with laws to kill it had killed it.

in epistles wherein i'm no god, my lens faults to
                        a click of
            misclick, a "Yes, I agree" with
me thus colonizing my damned
me. delusions of RAM, like grandeur, wherein a "he"

            placed his dimmed
blueprint totalitarian, his framework's shadow —
prisons with laws for
someone loved;

            it colored me so   well, every body
loved became censored
            black. bodies, which rods & cones were forced to render: forced-
            entered,

became broken to silent members alongside m[in]e —

as in, let's not talk about the

subject
of this poem, let's not talk about the subject of her body or
any deer as a metaphor for mine   let's not talk about what
it is to be here just governed   into a body   let alone
a governing body. can you smell the blood of this new lecture
about tacit consent? let's not talk about the idea of choice
let alone the talk of "lesser of two evils". in the laments
wherein you find me, evil consumed me so well it defined me,
so i [engirdled 'just got married' round his neck, i tied the knot with
my car, and i] killed me on my drive to objectively 'good now'
from a 'bad place'. i's a widow now, a window with a letter
opener charged at the single letter, n. until shattered
free of self. perhaps i guess a good person says, me & i got
divorced. it was about time, it was by force. in all the poems,
wherein, you say, i mostly sell puns for the living, i find god

as mine,

bested

by me into m[in]e.

mourning the animals i store   in rooms
inside me was civic duty. was the tax i paid
to love; the wager, not which at
any attainable time, could i, my deer, afford.

american sonnet for the terrains black Boy ghosts play on bare-foot, inside us

after Terrance Hayes

on days i haven't completely neglected the work of having
toes, i pray i'm dexterous enough to cartwheel & not paint the grass
with all my boy fumble   *should i want to hand these falls to science*
not silence?   poets are chemists, we know -- 'privilege catalysts for
'[e]x'; '[wh]y' is how my body triggers on the inside' -- but i know
some obsessed with how a world waits once it collides with another.
often my eyes are crashed worlds beneath skull, its cap often my sky,
& what stores itself behind my iris is moon quiet. perhaps
mountains mean to be mountains inside, under the eye - this is why
we shutter, shut out, shiver, cry: himalayan salts. at least *here*
when my bad boys nudge earth, the sound of dirt cannot deny i am
the world. we swung from off its guide, bent on forgiving the unknown
space, the   near nothing cupping infinitesimal dark; *from*   , *whose God*
heard the novas spark noise? i need my bad boys out; to know what's here.

carefree black / ghost peering beyond two masks

yes, i am

soft in the meantime   the interim in
electron & absence, of course
i don't care for strength.
i mourn, yes, my mouth.
i read black lips, peer, & see the grammar -
broken. my tongue dragged
by ankles
     with english
soon as i ask   *wusgood, sambo?*
i wade, perched north beneath a roof
as stalactites in the interim, the
cavernous english dark inside my mouth.
i become (*because why not?*) a long pitch black tunnel
rivered underwater between
African & American,
whose manta rays & Cuttlefish disperse & hover

the hyphen, like Atlantic oceanic mantle
inside black people, yet relinquished   in
the interim, we drink a bottle full of endless;
all the drowned names name themselves monks
of the caves inside
amongst themselves too early. in the interim, we
blow out the speakers & haze like philosophers in
Southside Jamaica. in Southside,
     maybe we speak the english that
learned to get along with itself. you know
i laugh at the idea of laughing, these things which we
cackle involuntary at;

perhaps, given we speak language
we ain't supposed to speak,
white men know we must know there is
some type of peace *here*
they can't perform. hey, maybe when i say
  wus crackin other than yo lips, negro?
     white men start
inquiring for the human tender enough to
grieve the dark body in its hands still damp
from genocide, hoping i won't take him
to how my mouth got this way, how i took

42

back english, how i make it mourn itself
for birthing

sambo' like me. how i crush phonetics
behind latin script behind my molars
& make the syllable crash into self.

white men don't know i'm only soft spoken
for now. they don't understand how i could
still take my time, since they ain't kno
time is mine.

they ain't kno how often i had to be ________
to endure the odds of it happening – all of the
atoms within the slave at the brim of becoming
water; allied powers gleaming their choice

when sour, their white horse gallops
toward my body, rippling crests in my
now cracked-open dialect in each dialectic.
                here, 400 years
unsheathed hairs of a mare thickened ripe with
invasion, his hooves painted each black lip
burgundy & whinnied an undoing. they ain't kno

how i once told my

death
wusgood?

what you doin here? i see you,
cowboy. where you
bout to be out to?
where we finna go?

smiles & other pronounced marks

nina sang. we walk from the table when
love's no longer being served &
the pain out of her note taught me this/hurt.

each time i bring myself to sit next to a table,
i ask *where am i?* i enunciate > then *now*
& bring dot to all of the *i* with a kind of calm
which won't make my aunt's room uncomfortable.
my aunt pat has had that same table all
my life - the four chairs around it made up
of cold, rusted iron & memory difficult
to swallow - the reason i can't do pills.

& if i recall correctly my first ass-whooping,
i once, as a five year-old would, fumbled
through a word that had required front teeth,
        "that".   but, first
ode to the belt who suggests we undress
when we have made a mistake &
would not tell us the mistake yet
would also fumble. like a jealous God
with her name caught wet in between
her fingers, aunt pat's love dragged me
naked across her lap as boy.
i think this was when i realized i was
boy
        - naked, ashy hands uncupping
what rendered me "boy", noting it
for this first time, & awaiting
somebody else's power to mark me
into a boy that knew this. pain.
        the belt said
that.   *that. that. that. that.*
did.n't. i. tell. you. the. word. is. that.
how. man.y. times. i. got.ta. tell. you.
that. for. you. to.   learn.
her belt once broke in my bathtime.
i wet myself yellow while nosediving
further in the playful soapy water,
each time the leather kissed my back.

i can't recall each summer spent

sunbathing in the sting of her, thinking
i was gonna get hit, whether or not
if she was angry, or if she was there
but, i remember how naked & often i was
red in rooms around me. i remember
one room, its too-many smiling portraits
in a glass cabinet. i remember

how a manicure dug when it had tried to get me
to swallow pills, so jammed-well in my face
i don't need recalling. some scars always
stay. as i remember the vomit, i remember
unbuttoning. i remember reasons
i would make up for getting smacked so fast
i became   the roar of bombs which
the belt aptly named   *discipline.*

some days there won't be an answer to why
i was beat. but i suppose my body always needs
one anyway. i return to singing Selsun blues,
in silence, soap drying out the dried scalp
& question marks off of my skin. pityriasis,
a [dermis] condition i once sat with, derived from
the stress of *who knows if the marks were made,
or who made them, or if it made me?* but,

to move on: grandma says   *you look
too much like her brother,*   that's why.
my ass just says   *damn.*   it once said
   *what   can   i give you
        for all this to be   over?   here.
                have it   here
          it's. yours.   here
   take it. please. go.   here.*

ode to pokemon trainer Red

(B)   has always taught me to run
whether it be from a pokemon battle or an
unexpected visit from an actual bee's noise.
i **(B)** run up stairs

like i'm sure to see my father. & i am not his,
just mine, & my thick hair twists, once in, now,
just now, an unrivalled out.   i barely
care about what he thinks about my hair,

the ones i love, the way i dress, the way i give love,
          as i would barely,
remember my Nintendo DS Lite. how it don't
work no more 'cause it had guillotined to
divorce right after the charger had broke.
i do remember
          Ranger, & Platinum, & Diamond,
riddled quiet in dusted cases; each
pokemon game & cartridge i
had as all i had
                    when
my father wasn't there.   & when my son,
Mew, reached level 100, i had made the best of
the hand   *Oak*   dealt me.   *Red, Ash, &*
Silver
          all dreamt my dream for a father
& i remember how they all never spoke. & i
remember whichever name you gave him

becoming the boy's name. Silver's mom got
those running shoes from Silver's dad.
Silver once ran into a cave atop a mountain
          & then found him - Red,
          at its precipice,
                    transforming into,
          now, just now, a Mew

- with its hair returned untethered & to
 its original form; & so mindful
a Mew, in fact, he did learn how to learn
any move so one
          might be performed like a dance which

46

might serve, like a mating call, to summon
          a father who too   searches for father.

remember? that conflict with Mew. once led
ash's heart to petrified stone in the stale air. &
how diamond should sublimate to stale air,
a Pikachu's tear once hauled Ash from his
cryogenesis, in fact, so well - Ash hasn't aged
since, which implies Ash could die & get born
again & still have no father. we all remember

waking up alone & to a new mother, saying
          not a thing
          has changed,   not our father,   not
our mountains,   not Pokemon."
     as fathers go unmentioned in the games
     until 2002,   my dad & i still don't talk.
i wonder about how much it has to do with

being a father.   i go to capture
a moment's truth & stick it in poems
as trainers **(B)** run to catch the Mewtwo
                    with just pokeballs.
i hope Red had taken time to write (t)his
requiem for his lost dad, when trainer
Silver, had happened
to find him praying at the mountain froth.

perhaps Red caught a cold & this
father-poem needed to be about how cold &
alone Red felt. maybe his throat
hurt too much to talk so Red fled the fight
               in hopes to get a healing with
his father. maybe it was less of a **(B)** run &
moreso **(A)** jump; that his father was just
a sky away. just now.
               i **(B)** run up stairs like i will
see my own. in the sky. from the top step
of mountains until i'm downstairs
with my single momma again...

band-aids & other temporary healings

i don't think there comes inherent healing
        with poems or with time.

i was so triggered i thought i was home
i got comfortable i took off my bag, jacket,
    each layer   down from my shoulder
until i unzipped & was sitting on my own skin
    in the dark so long
it could only have been a chair,   wherein
my skin hangs   ass over armrest
for decoration,   growing eyes out in
    this silence, like a passive God,
and yet everything   was just   still there/*here*,
                                            like my
eczema, from which i scrape so long, i
        pull, from scabs, scaffold with your bike
attached near my projects' building.
        yes, i did   thumb through all this/his
                    courtcase/heartbreak/belt
which made this brown a darker brown

i said *it fertilized my flower bed on some days*,
        knowing some days that it would not.
&, yes, this whole thing's a garden. this *it*,
or itch, the scaffold contraption, with its
chains, lock,

& self,   clung to iron
        like how mothers do
the good baby after losing custody   i'd say
each bike, hugging the scaffold, was, is, me.
        and it "was", in the poem, *here* -

        i asked to be let out of me
so long in that room   in the interim,

boy got his wish for death, got born again,
woke up in a new mother's arms, & then,
he handed us his newest intercom

48

eulogy. & though we know each
mother wants every moment he could have
been to rupture all the eardrums
     of a passive God,   all we asked for was
a moment/of silence. we's counterintuitive.
but, this,   this one time i died for so long,
while i became a quantum thing
so broken in its compartments
light can't emit, i thought i was giving
out a healing/a poem/a love but fell instead
and kept falling until   every orifice of me
had shifted   to red
and then translucent and   then, *yasssss...*
but wait ... *what*
  was his name? whomever he was, was he
who i was then? *here* giving empty space,
paradoxically warm, with a mouth
so good, God undid me. and i̶ kept going.
knowing all that i wanted was
a whole body again,   all i asked for
was   to be/undone.

how mother dusting off her son's casket,
with wail, begins to have an a'ight day,
within an archive of stillness & still-
together, i am still/*here*, there.

Mike Brown is eighteen

[and legal]   *now,* [taking full advantage
of the simply enough he is.
might just go sign up for the war.
might as well.

can't get drunk,
or get a real loan
without his parents' death offered,
as if it were even legal
to be young, and black, and living
and really living.
he's no exception.
he's just "legal"   now:

legal to sex and war and sign
permission slips, as his new guardian
for his own intents,
now, and purposes.

what is young black life?
but, thick hair,
them good organs for the taking,
and crying mothers,
anyhow. any when. anyway, if that. then, what
makes him feel
he even had the right to be
rendered as enough?

to be black, undead, and worthy
of the space we take
up feels paradoxical now
and then;

his only constant
his own long-forgotten privilege
to have been born heir
to surplus, *here,* of self-doubt.
but, he's legal now,
old enough to be
declared … *'nough of that.*
and withstand it all.]
    might as well…

[...]

~~(ALARM TIME:)~~ ~~[once after, I hope,...]~~
                                I learn   to
              [love] / process...

To those with the most
overt *liberty*
in a land where all but us have
freedom,

(In this land: of cages wherein
this *here*
the only given, you are
born dead, thus:)

The blu[es]est song in
you was optical illusion.
You so angry you
could only cry so
much so you had thought
              *

you were sad like God
52

finding out that "He"
itself had been dead
for months, convinced 'his'
own blood was the sky,
& burgundy now
the truest saddest
blues: now this is only a red-
shift:

Such a stunned old boy's
response it all was even then,
even 'his' own phallus
emptied for itself on himself
"Look! Silly, you flinch
when anyone touches your chest
but you." (& because
your love's hands revealed
this fact, you tell them,
your love, in response

 "hands at the sternum
make a broken heart feel like an
   empty room
for even the smallest petals of love

& every piece of room inside
might illuminate just for this"

She, the girl that loved
his problem, tried to
wipe the whitest cloud
off your chest's cage) &
the sky was under-
neath you underneath
her hands: this is how
she would wash you each
eon: translucent.
                *
You (- bathe in privilege,
blink, & then, you are
no longer bathing
but sunbathing now
in this cage that a love can be;
            You) - now her,
now his God,

are at watching "He"
who wrote *here*, all the
this thus far, about
you, wherein "he" has
referred to you as
'you' & clearly, nothing of it
here makes sense because
you know only intangible
things make a real God's
miracle noise in befuddled,
dark, little gardens perpetually
unmade *here* as 'him.'
~~(this death of all you~~
~~had known to be true~~
~~——————————— is joy,~~
~~so much even the~~
~~pronoun itself, was dead &~~
~~did not, could not, have~~
~~been acknowledged in~~
~~all of whatever that black, on~~
~~burgundy, thing or~~
~~thought, was. & you smiled.~~
~~Oh,~~ what it must have been
for him for you to
have blinked & for him to
have just missed a laugh
that was yours, 'hers,' that
was within 'him': The
pronoun) 'he' might have
been dead this entire time it
took to get here. Yes,

that would explain the
weeping willows hung
within 'his' lungs, which
you saw blossom as a breeze
before you & fall back into
an asymptote sky until 'his'
cape, *it / now / here*, curved 400
years as an upside-
down garden, at which
you nearly cackled.
*

A <u>garden</u> –

wherein, after 'his' first-ever
blink, it was named Love

& it was as it
[- was, cascading it-
self from beneath us
to beyond (just a bit beyond)
that, & in the same
space *here* wherein the 2nd time
'he' would ever blink,
it would be last time
'he' would ever blink,
& was, then, looking
up from within this:
carved out poplar tree,
now for some reason
beneath the soil: 6 feet – for
you, as Love, with 'he'
with such little power, in your
hands, like fruit that were
so strange[...(... its crop, like
a carrot with roots
to its heavens, *here*, quantum
spinning since never
belonging to the world & was
effacing of it,)...]ly black, 'he'
was introduced to
            his' own
~~family~~ heartbreak of
death before 'he' met
even 'his' first diastole for the
first time, back when 'he'
made somebody else God,
back then in this one moment,
'he' knew, like rhythm,
God was real. But then,
sadly, in a fleeting breath, you,
still 'his' first, only
God, spoke within 'him'
this, boy, is not, won't be, enough…
say what you mean &...,
for the first time you,
God, left, silently becoming
the night, like most 'men'
in a room in dirt, or in life,

as passive as it is to laugh.
'he' - for the last time,
felt 'he' was never
enough since 'his' birth,
at least not for anyone's want,
ever, not since 'he'
was told so well of
this pain, 'he' knew, in
fact, you, as Love, too
were once dead & that, perhaps, one of us
here is heaven if we still had
the freedom to just act on that
want: or perhaps 'he'
assumed you just knew,
as you were 'his' God,
even if he felt free to act on
a want, a piece of room inside
'Him' was, yes, a slave
inside: the garden —
He[re;] sprouting tombstone
petals -] was just, in
Layman's English, a

plantation,

or what is a cemetery
called when not one thing
in it, not even itself, has
a name? A tall tale?
A chest emptied of lies into
a sky that may have truly just
been his own backwards
blood? The tallest, silliest, tale?

*

&, as backwards as it was to
not act on a want, this lament
of question declares
'his' death must have came
before 'his' lifecycle for 'him'
to know it so well —

even before 'he' bloomed,
~~[& became alive as Lazarus.~~
~~You see this. You see~~
~~'him' try to love it~~
~~self, despite when 'he'~~
56

~~was not enough to change any~~
~~of this death(but was~~
~~black enough to have~~
~~swallowed his countless~~
~~brothers countless deaths,~~
~~during which 'he',~~
~~or any man's white imaginary,~~
~~falls in & out of li[f]e's cage, &~~
~~almost~~ ————
          like syruping in
between laps of binary of 'he'
& you, his Love, his
God, us, our Love,
& death, with intents only of
Being. That intent)]: This
imagined joy of
'his' - that was when 'he'
made somebody into a God
who was not:

You, still God, still Love
as *here* as a God can be, ask
to this broken-dead
pronoun that *a broken 'him' is*
just as much a hymn too dead too
sing as the pronoun 'he' is just
not enough, since any black 'he'
can be an oppressed
oppressor, both unaware &/
or aware of this, & that, here,
is a privilege that he has which
you, dear Love, do not
since you are not man's
or man here[..., asking
"...*Why would anyone trust a black*
'him' that even sings of God? &
unless 'he' is in fact this God,
Why are we convinced
'His' hymn conjures anything like
one?"] - This *coming* is
what 'he' thought happened
when 'he' emptied him-
self of himself: Blood:
Blood with no heaven
& no end, once these questions had began:

again, that, to him-
self, he thought was what
 it was like to be
a thing relinquished
of power
            [, as the dominant
male resident, in a nation
 of citizens *here*, sharing, as
oppressed oppressor
& twice & the tertiary
oppressed now together, in a
most overt *liberty* in this
plot of stolen land
where still all else have
freedom & we, together, still
do not (since we are
never citizens where we once,
now & forever, here, considered a property:
here - a time & space
wherein the heaven
for black pronouns is
forbidden for as long as they
speak with a language
which had been devoid,
originally, of blackness.)
                        *
You read 'him'
like the narrative of water.
You get 'him']. You say
(to that dead 'he' with
a barrage
of bullets' boutonniere)   ...*Silly,*
I love you.
You are not allowed to leave me
until you
say what you mean, &
mean what you say, &
& don't say it mean.

('he' then says, to itself,
this too, as shackles
around the pronoun
itself undo into dust &
then death,)

58

as if to imply   take my hand,
boy.
pull from here enough
so you are so full
you once thought you were
drowning but,
know now you were not,
& you wake up from
death:

You kiss hymn, her, whom-
ever you are, yourself.
You, to yourself, say I love you,
okay? I'm so sorry:

*

this is what it's like
for that son's sun to
give light to your skies'
blood in that nipple
pricked from Southern time,
when expanding   in-
to nothings of space –
it was the kind of nothing that
should vibrate between
you & death & yet,
like a rattling in Kalief's
cages of li[f]e, of ribs, of state,
have nothing react
(- it was like looking at a God
trying to look for itself, so
lost in everyone
that everything, all
at once, even the walls inside
the rooms placed in 'his'
without-home body,
shattered, still shattering into
the outside cage of 'him' like a
slave's song, in attempt
to create just a mirror, &
what was left of 'his'
sternum resembled Atlantic
Oceans' worth of what
it took to get this far; its kind
of unbecoming left shrapnel
so small, so redundant, it will

only be called a _hyphen_ - that
blue, that clear, that much
can be in a cage
broken like windows' approach to freedom:
falling, upwards even, but, still,
falling short.
& the throbbing air
outside 'his' wounded
body, in the earth
of this casket, (which
was a cage which was
a tree, _here,_ inside
this: another cage which
was once just all trees,)
became what
we, good folk, defined
as shelter, or even the word
world, itself) -
You wish.

       You think you
should so you

pray "I hope I learn
                      to love

process."

This, all of it, again, only to say

I hope I will love all of me
& all of those that look] like me...

within an almost
nervous laugh, _here._ &
this(,) you(,) begins, here.(..

       .... somewhat, after this.)

[P.S.:
       "this" which means to ask:
is _this_ love [enough]? is it [_here_]?

60

Acknowledgments

Several poems have appeared with the following journals, anthologies, &
other homes. Thank you,

    Scholastic Art & Writing Awards, NPR's The Takeaway: "Silence"
Split This Rock: "Mike Brown is Eighteen"
Entropy Magazine, BET Next Level: "father's isolation & i"
Black Heart Magazine: "when to (k)not"
The Poetry Breakfast: "Open Letter to Dymel"
I Come From The World: "How we keep time/during Kwanzaa",
"Agenda for the codependent lover"
    Black Napkin Press: "Band-Aids & other temporary healings",
"the other day"
    Wusgood? Magazine: "When Black Men Want to Leave"
Smuggler: "Band-Aids & other temporary healings" (short film)
Great Weather For Media's 'The Other Side of Violet' Anthology:
"[requiem] for the boy telling of the time his body was not his"
    Penmanship Books' Voices of the East Coast Anthology - "lament of
the slave who does not jump"
    Anamolous Press: "Requiem for the butterfly effect", "The tesseract
tethers rooms", and "Carefree black / ghost peering beyond two masks"

So many, whom I may not be here without, have blessed me with their
ears, their insight, and the warmth of their own company. For listening &
for rooting for me, you will always have a place within me,
+
to my dear friends: Francena Jimenez, Jonathan Gachette, Bobb Alexander,
Akeil Davis, Rahni Davis, Kearah Armonie, Sore Agbaje, Carmin Wong,
Nkosi Nkululeko, Gabriel Ramirez, Terron Davis, Dwayne Moore, Stara-
sia Wright, Mr. Lagmay, Ms. Petroutsos, Maassai Sade, IS Jones, Robyn
Forgie, Assata Alston, Afolami Fasanya & Mikal Lee, thank you.

my Udub fam: Ashley August, Aziza Barnes, Jon Sands, Jose Olivarez,
Safiya Martinez, Sofia Snow, Shannon Matesky, Jive, Khadjiah, Penda,
Will, Khalin, Aaya, Imani, Sergio, Mahlaney, Juliana, Gurkirat, Esther,

Makayla, Crystal, Ramya, DJ Mega, Jadon, Savon, Lady Logic, Adam Falkner, Carvens Lissaint, Miles Hodges, Joshua Bennett, Timothy Du-White, Jayson Smith, Angel Nafis, Maya Osborne, Roya Marsh, Steven Willis, Mahogany L. Browne & Aja Monet, thank you.
to Lauren Whitehead, Kristina Grimlich, Leslie Lissaint, & the cast of "How Bodies Reclaim Light", thank you.

my Aunt Nonie, Aunt Janet, Ms, Brenda, Ms. Ava, Ms. Pat, Karen Hart-well, Aunt Reese, Che, Chance, Amenophis, Nicole Lawrence, Grandma Ree, Aunt Cheryl, Aunt Jessica, Cheryl Boyce-Taylor, DJ Renegade, & my DePass family, & to Antonio, Tendo, Hannah, Sazia, Corianna, & the good folks at the Scholastic A&W Awards, thank you all.
to my mom, my grandmother, & to all those who create spaces wherein poems like these might find shelter, thank you.

& to PANK Books for tirelessly believing in this work, thank you.

& to you, of course, thank you.